CLASSIC GUITAR   Compiled & E

COMPLETE GIULIANI STUDIES

David Grimes uses and endorses LaBella strings.

WWW.MELBAY.COM

CONTENTS

INTRODUCTION

The studies of Mauro Giuliani stand alongside those of Fernando Sor, Matteo Carcassi, Dionisio Aguado and Ferdinando Carulli as the staples of the didactic pieces by the "first generation" of classical guitarists. The six-string guitar (what we now call the "classical" guitar) was a new development in the late eighteenth century, and a number of talented guitarist/composers set about exploring the capabilities of their chosen instrument and providing learning pieces for students and amateurs.

Mauro Giuliani (1781-1829) was one of the most celebrated guitarists of his age - a brilliant performer and a prolific composer. He left an extensive legacy of compositions, and many of his works are heard regularly in recitals and concerts today. In addition to his concert works, Giuliani composed numerous studies and other pieces intended for students and amateurs, and these have been considered indispensable by generations of guitarists.

There is often an indistinct dividing line between "studies" and other short compositions, and many composers have called pieces "studies" seemingly for lack of more suitable titles. Giuliani's studies usually have clearly-defined pedagogical purposes. Giuliani also wrote a number of other works intended for amateurs and less-advanced players, calling them "divertissements" or "amusements," and these are listed with the studies in Thomas Heck's seminal dissertation on Giuliani, The Birth of the Classic Guitar and its Cultivation in Vienna, Reflected in the Career and Compositions of Mauro Giuliani, Yale University, 1970. Giuliani did not choose to call these pieces studies, however, and they have not been included here, although they are certainly recommended for use by all students. Opus 50, "Le Papillon," in particular, contains excellent material for beginning students.

The studies and exercises contained in the six opus numbers here provide some of the most effective material in the entire guitar literature for building and refining a superior technical command of the guitar. In this edition I have modernized some of the notation and corrected a number of misprints.

In Opus 139 and in the first three Parts of Opus 1, Giuliani provided detailed fingering instructions, while in Opus 48 and Opus 100 he indicated only position numbers (Roman numerals), and in Opus 51 and Opus 98 he offered no fingerings at all. Since these works are intended for student use, I have suggested supplemental fingerings to help solve some problems and to help lay the foundations for good fingering habits. Where Giuliani specified fingerings, I have tried to respect the musical concepts, altering fingerings only where contemporary practice offers smoother and more efficient left-hand use. I have also omitted some of the superfluous fingerings in Part Three of Opus 1.

NOTES

Giuliani's Opus 1 is made up of four parts and constitutes a most useful summation of Giuliani's technical ideas. Part One is well known as the famous (or infamous) 120 Daily Studies that use various right-hand arpeggio formulae on basic C and G7 chords. These have been used with good results by students and teachers for many years. Unjustly neglected, however, are the other sections of Opus 1. The interval studies in Part Two are among the very most effective left-hand studies in the literature, and the studies in articulations, damping, slurs and ornaments in Part Three are highly pertinent and useful.

Giuliani's meticulous and detailed fingerings in Opus 1 deserve close attention and study. In the interval studies it is clear that he preferred to keep the left hand in one fingerboard position, using finger movements across the strings, rather than (perhaps more "naturally") sliding along the fingerboard with the stronger fingers. The fingering of a particular passage in a piece to be performed is entirely situational, depending upon the musical content, and Giuliani used other systems in his fingering for other pieces. In Opus 139, No. 3, for instance, the original fingering calls for the parallel thirds to be fingered by sliding the first finger along the first string, in direct contradiction to the advice proffered in Opus 1. Giuliani's consistent approach in the Opus 1 interval studies, however, provides exceptional exercise for strengthening and equalizing the fingers and promotes smooth cooperation among them. I have revised the original fingerings somewhat in a number of cases in accordance with contemporary practice and to clarify the concept of efficient fingering. Giuliani also used the left-hand thumb to stop some notes on the sixth string, and this has required some fingering revisions. In these interval studies, the left hand should prepare both notes of the interval at the same time, training the fingers to work in coordinated pairs.

The 24 short pieces in Opus 48 present an excellent preparatory course for playing and interpreting Giuliani's concert works. They contain many of the figurations, textures and technical problems that will appear frequently in the performing repertoire. In fact, several of the studies in Opus 48 are excerpted directly from passages in a number of Giuliani's concert works. Study 16, for instance, is identical (apart from a few inconsequential details and the final cadence) with measures 209 - 242 in the first movement of Giuliani's "Grand Concerto," Opus 30.

Opus 51 is a progressive set of studies for beginning-to-intermediate guitarists. Several of the pieces are quite familiar to teachers, offering examples of technical and musical situations that will be found frequently in the music of Giuliani's time.

As the title indicates, the eight pieces that make up Opus 98 are entertaining and pleasant, but have somewhat less focus as pedagogical material. The difficulty level is early intermediate.

Opus 100 contains four types of studies. The first nine pieces are studies in arpeggios over chords forming typical harmonic progressions in keys with up to four sharps or flats. The next seven are short caprices and rondos, and the concluding section contains "Preludes to use as cadenzas before beginning a piece of music" in the keys most commonly used in 19th-century guitar music.

The title page of Opus 139 advertises 24 pieces in four volumes "for the use of amateurs who want to improve without the aid of a teacher." Only the first volume (six pieces) is now extant.

As noted above, Giuliani's smaller guitar allowed him to stop some bass notes by wrapping his left thumb around the narrower fingerboard to the sixth string. In pieces in the key of F, Giuliani occasionally wrote the final six-string chord (in first position) with an open low A, barring only the first two strings and stopping the low F with the thumb. On a modern guitar this causes an unsatisfactory deviation from good hand position and is no longer accepted in standard technique. In those chords I have replaced the low A with the C on the fifth string. (The final chord in Opus 1, Part 4, Number 9 is one example.)

Giuliani was not averse to using "unusual" or "backward" fingerings when the occasion called for creative solutions to fingering problems. In Op. 1, Part 3, No. 2, for instance, a "backward" fingering (that is actually fairly standard) is seen in line 1, measure 2, where the third finger is left on the low C while the second finger plays the F on the fourth string. This is more efficient than reorganizing the fingers to a more "natural" disposition.

In Opus 100, No. 4, a fingering problem arises in line 9, measures 1 and 3. Here Giuliani would most likely have used his left thumb to stop the low F sharp in the last beat; the most viable modern option is to use a "slant bar," with the first finger laid diagonally across the fingerboard from the E sharp on the first string to the F sharp on the sixth.

Many guitarists in Giuliani's time used ligados (slurs) for almost all scalar lines, and the general practice was to place dots above or below the notes that were **not** to be slurred. Such a dot attached to a note now signifies a definite staccato, and I have removed Giuliani's articulation dots to avoid confusion. The notated slurs and the fingerings given are sufficient to specify the intent clearly.

Giuliani applied sforzando signs to many notes that would seem to require only moderate stress. In most cases, these merely point out appoggiaturas or other dissonances, which should be given more weight than their following resolutions. He also used this notation occasionally to emphasize dominant-to-tonic relationships. In similar cases in other pieces, the same effect is indicated by short decrescendo "hairpins." Either of these indications will help to clarify the musical direction for students, and both have been retained.

The original editions of Giuliani's studies contain relatively few errors (missing beams, missing accidentals, clearly wrong notes, etc.). Most of these are obvious and have been corrected here without individual comment. In a number of instances, however, I have felt that there were some not-quite-so-obvious errors, and the changes I have made are listed below.

Op. 1, Part 4, No. 2 (p. 48) - line 4, measure 1: the third note was printed as C, not D.
Op. 1, Part 4, No. 11 (p. 57) - l. 9, m. 3: the first up-stem was printed as E, not C sharp.
Op. 1, Part 4, No. 12 (p. 58) - l. 5, m. 2: the last note was printed as E, not F sharp.

Op. 48, No. 5 (p. 63) - l. 5, m. 1: in beat three, the first and last up-stems were printed as A's, not B's. In beat four, the D sharps were printed as E's.
Op. 48, No. 16, page two (p. 77) - l. 5, m. 1: the first down-stem was shown as E, not C sharp.
Op. 48, No. 17, page two (p. 79) - l. 6, m. 1: the first two up-stem G's were printed as B flats.

Op. 51, No. 7 (p. 97) - l. 2, m. 3: the sharp sign for the G was missing.
Op. 51, No. 9 (p. 99) - l. 4, m. 2: the first up-stem was printed as C, not A.
Op. 51, No. 16 (p. 106) - l. 7, m. 2: the last three treble C's were printed as E.
    - l. 9, m. 2: the sixth note was printed as C, not B.

Op. 98, No. 2 (p. 114) - l. 7, m. 4: the first eighth note was printed as A, not G.
Op. 98, No. 4 (p. 118) - l. 4, m. 5: the down-stem G's were printed as A's.
    page two (p. 119) - l. 2, m. 4: the down-stem G's were printed as A's.
    page two (p. 119) - l. 7, m. 1: the third up-stem was printed as B, not C sharp.
Op. 98, No. 7, page two (p. 125) - l. 4, m. 5: the first up-stems were printed as B and D, not C and E.
Op. 98, No. 8, page two (p. 127) - l. 2, m. 2: the sharp sign for the A was missing.

Op. 100, No. 6 (p. 135) - l. 8, mm. 2 & 3: the last note was printed as F, not D.
Op. 100, No. 10 (p. 139) - l. 2, m. 3: the first note was printed as D, not E.
    - l. 8, m. 1: the last three notes were printed as F flat-G natural-F instead of A flat-B natural-A.
    - l. 9, m. 1: the fourth note was printed as B, not C.
Op. 100, No. 11 (p. 140) - l. 8, m. 1: the up-stem F's were printed as E's.
Op. 100, No. 13, page two (p. 145) - l. 3, m. 3: the natural sign was missing.
Op. 100, No. 14 (p. 146) - l. 5, m. 1: there was not natural sign in the original.
Op. 100, No. 15, page two (p. 149) - l. 6, m. 1: the second bass note was printed as B, not A.
Op. 100, No. 16, page two (p. 151) - l. 1, m. 1: the fourth down-stem was shown as A, not D.
Op. 100, No. 18 (p. 152) - l. 1: the twelfth note (G) was printed as a sixteenth, not an eighth.
Op. 100, No. 24 (p. 156) - l. 1, m. 3 and l. 2, m. 1: the first three up-stems were printed as C sharp-F sharp-A instead of F sharp-A-C sharp.

David Grimes
July, 1995

Studio per la Chitarra
(The Study of the Guitar)

Opus 1

Part One
Arpeggio exercises for the right hand

No. 1

No. 2

No. 3

No. 4

No. 5

No. 6

No. 7

No. 8

No. 9

No. 10

No. 11

No. 12

No. 13

No. 14

No. 15

No. 16

No. 17

No. 18

No. 19

No. 20

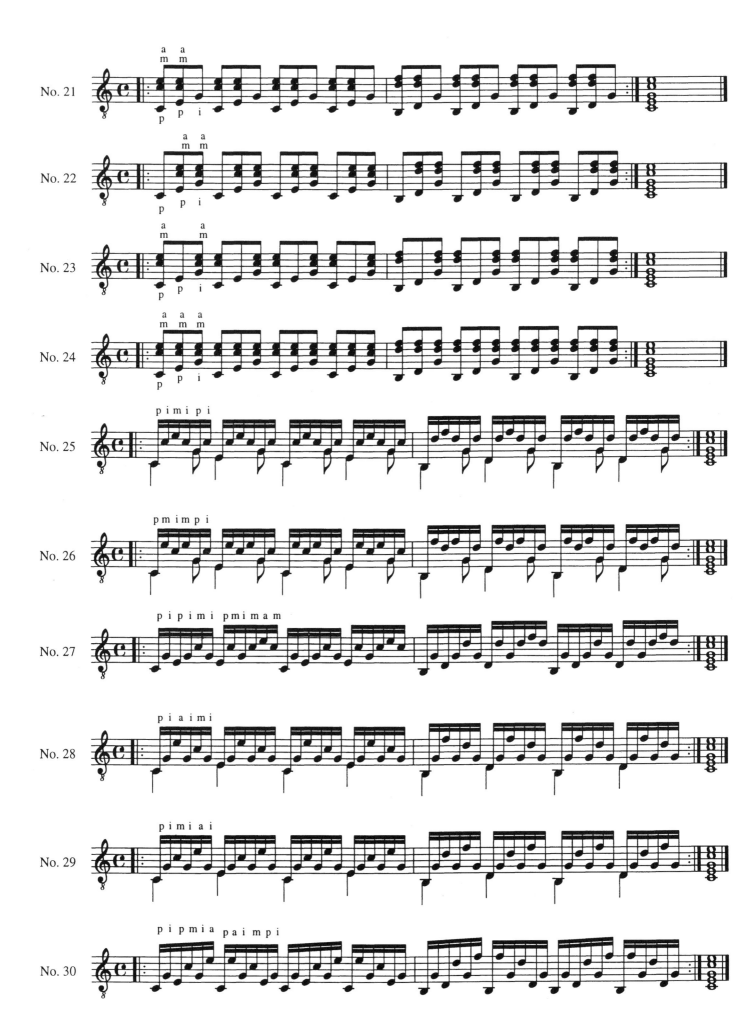

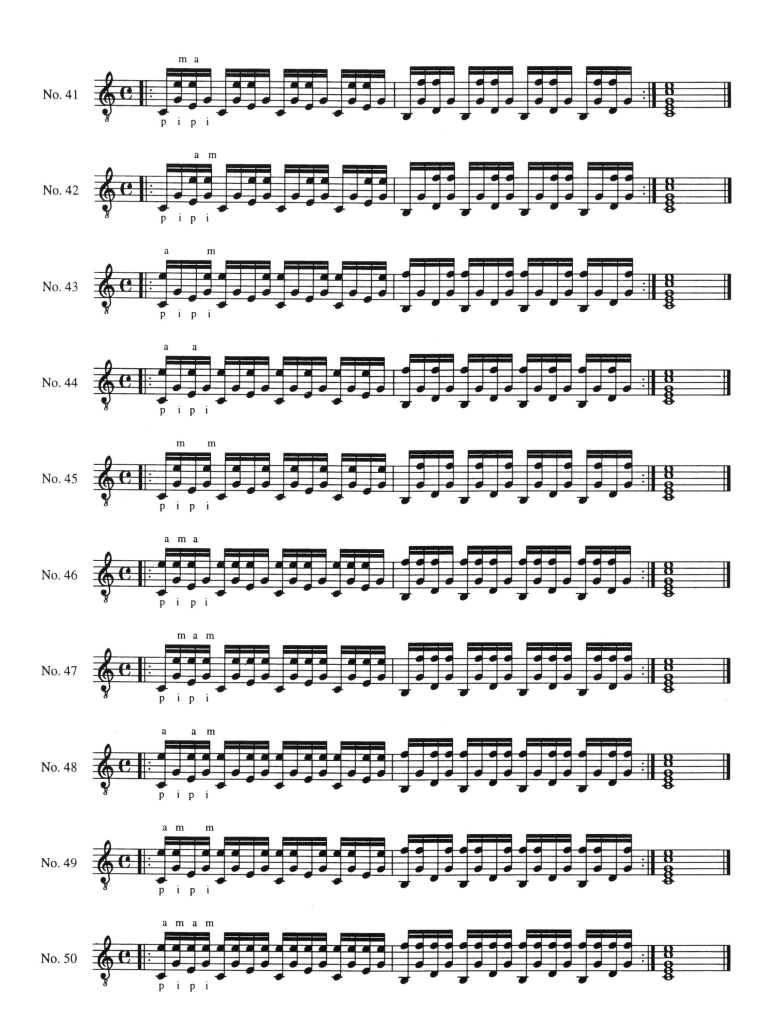

No. 41

No. 42

No. 43

No. 44

No. 45

No. 46

No. 47

No. 48

No. 49

No. 50

12

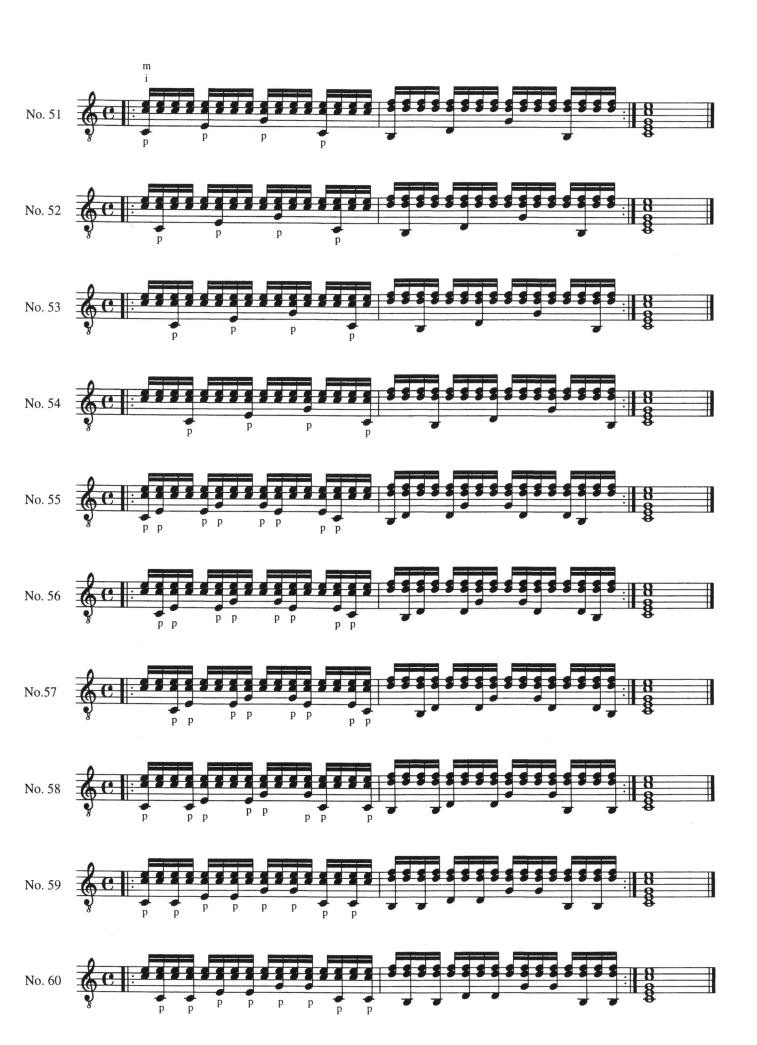

13

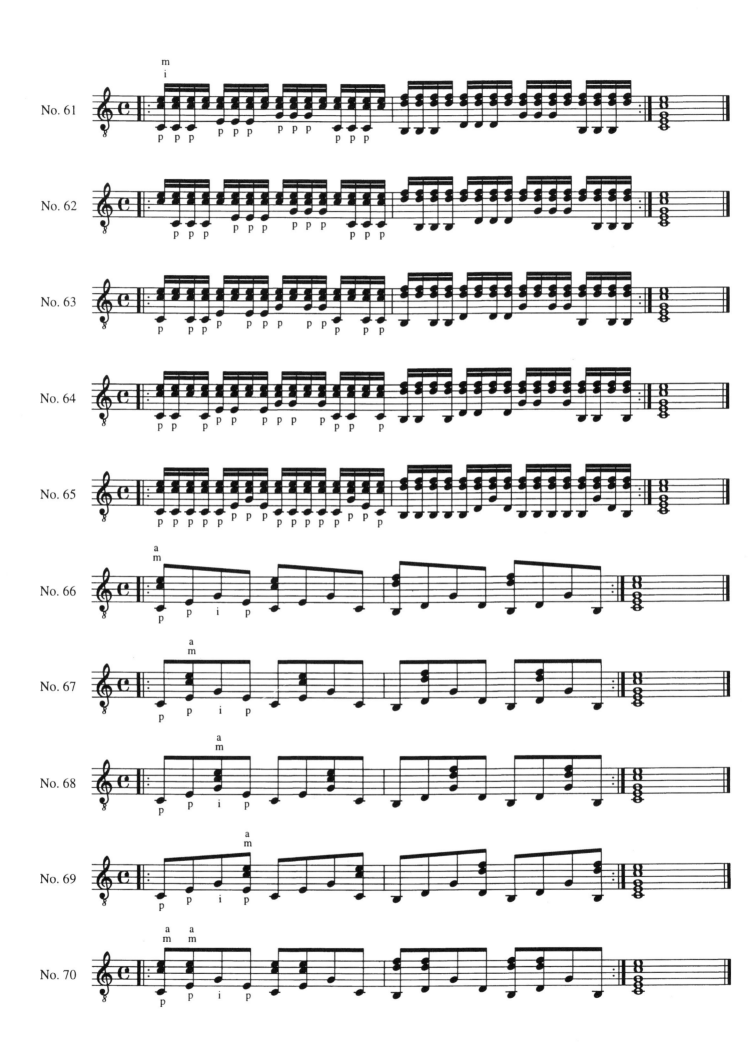

No. 61

No. 62

No. 63

No. 64

No. 65

No. 66

No. 67

No. 68

No. 69

No. 70

14

15

18

No. 111

No. 112

No. 113

No. 114

No. 115

No. 116

No. 117

No. 118

No. 119

No. 120

19

Part Two
Exercises in intervals for the left hand
Thirds in C major, up to the seventh position

No. 1

Sixths in C major, up to the eighth position

No. 2

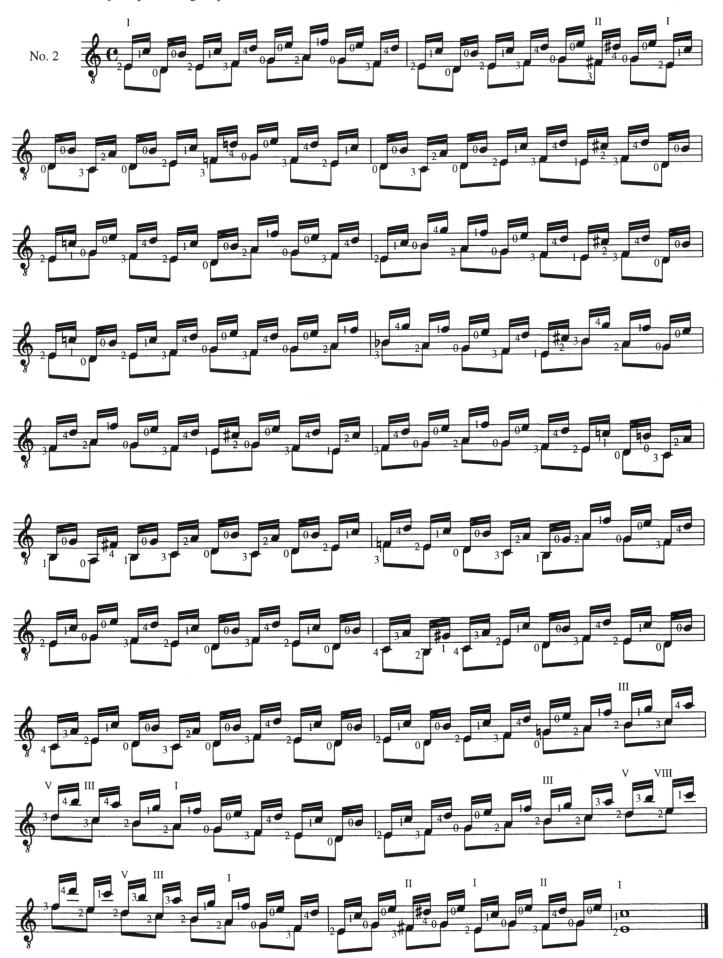

21

Octaves in C major, up to the fifth position

No. 3

Tenths in C major, up to the eleventh position

No. 4

Thirds in G major, up to the seventh position

No. 5

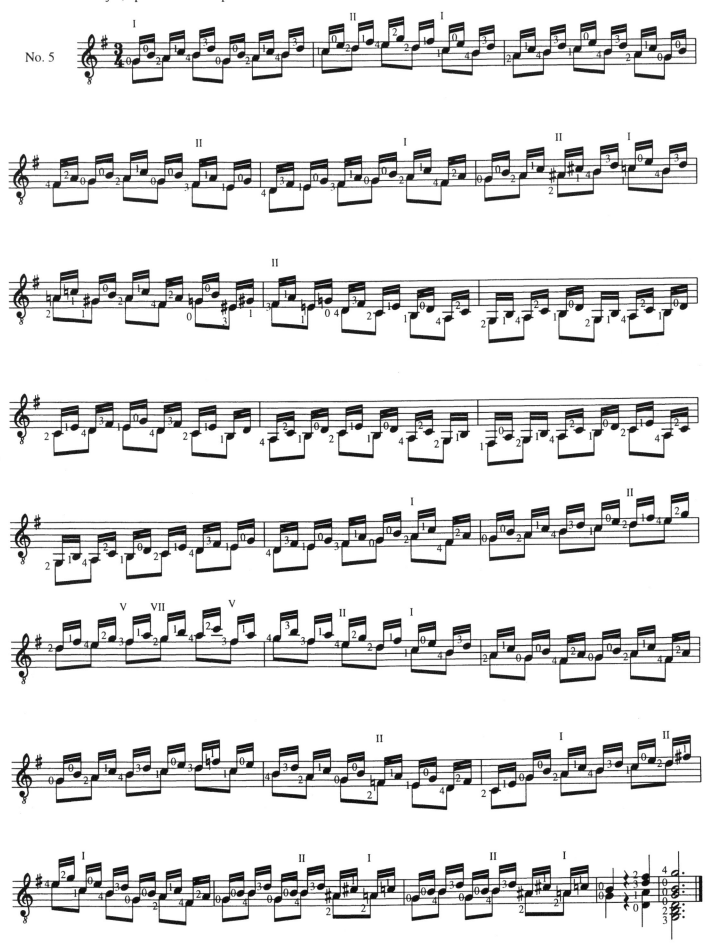

Sixths in G major, up to the seventh position

No. 6

Octaves in G major, up to the seventh position

Tenths in G major, up to the fifth position

No. 8

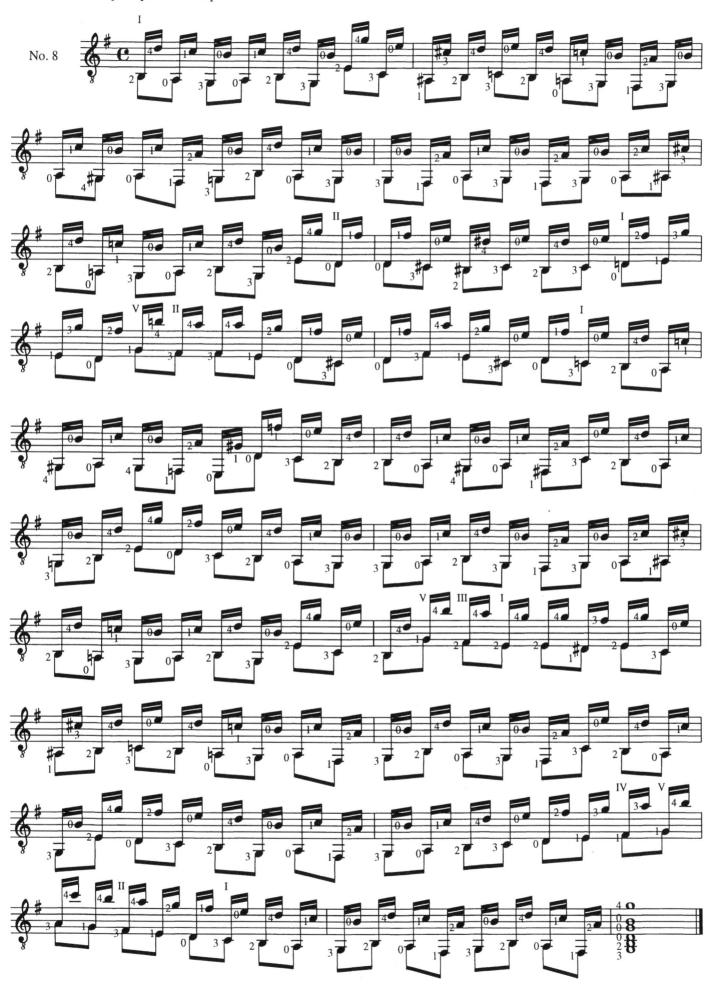

Thirds in D major, up to the ninth position

No. 9

28

Sixths in D major, up to the fifth position

No. 10

Octaves in D major, up to the seventh position

No. 11

30

Tenths in D major, up to the fifth position

Thirds in A major, up to the ninth position

No. 13

32

Sixths in A major, up to the ninth position

No. 14

33

Octaves in A major, up to the fourth position

No. 15

34

Tenths in A major, up to the eighth position

No. 16

Part Three
Exercises in articulation, damping, ligados and ornaments

A note is sustained by maintaining the pressure of the left-hand finger throughout the value of the note. This should be observed rigorously for the bass notes in this example.

Damping. After allowing the note to ring for its written value, damp the sound by touching the string with the same finger that plucked the note, since the slightest touch reduces the string to silence.

Articulation. For articulation of the greatest possible rapidity, avoiding right-hand fatigue from frequent finger repetition, the index and middle (and annular) fingers are used in alternation, as shown by the fingerings given below.

No. 3

Acciaccatura from below. To make the melody note sound sufficiently, the left-hand finger must "hammer" sharply (or slide) from the preceding note.

Acciaccatura from above. To link the grace note with the melody note, pluck the former with the right hand, then pluck the string horizontally with the left-hand finger that held the grace note.

An ornament with multiple notes. After the first of the two grace notes is plucked by the right hand, the left hand executes the next two notes as ascending ligados.

41

Another ornament with multiple notes (inverted mordent). A single left-hand finger executes an ascending ligado followed by a descending ligado.

Grupetto. Only the first note of the ornament is plucked with the right hand. The second note and the final note are played as descending ligados, while the third and fourth are played as ascending ligados.

No. 8

Acciaccatura. This much-used ornament is executed in the manner described in Example Five, plucking horizontally with a finger of the left hand.

Ascending ligado. The first note is plucked with the right hand, then the second is produced by a left-hand finger falling onto the string.

Glissando. After the small note is plucked, the left-hand finger that stops it slides to the melody note, sounding all the intervals in between, in the fashion of the ornament that singers call "portamento."

No. 12 Simple trill. After plucking a note with the right hand, strike the next higher note forcefully and repeatedly with a finger of the left hand, making both notes sound.

Simple trill

Two-string trill. This trill, which is preferable to the other since it sounds for the full value of the note, is played with the index and middle fingers or with the thumb and index of the right hand.

Two-string trill

Mordent. The mordent is nothing other than a short trill, executed in the same fashion. (NOTE: This is not the customary usage of the term "mordent" today.)

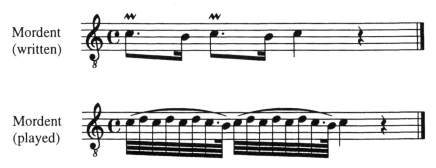

Mordent (written)

Mordent (played)

Part Four
Twelve Lessons

Maestoso

No. 1

No. 2

Allegretto grazioso

48

Andantino mosso

No. 3

No. 4

Allegro grazioso

50

No. 6

Allegretto con moto

Allegro maestoso

No. 7

53

Allegro spiritoso

No. 8

54

No. 10

Allegro spiritoso

Esercizio per la Chitarra
(Training for the Guitar)

Opus 48

No. 3

61

Moderato

No. 4

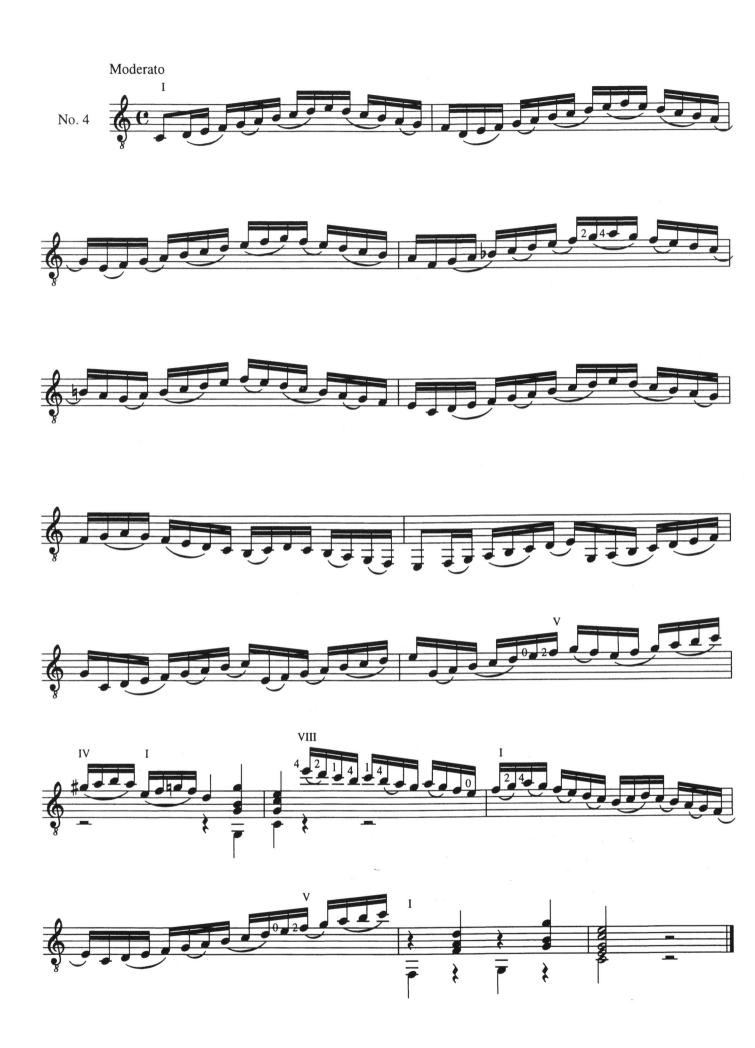

No. 5

Allegro

63

No. 6

64

Maestoso

No. 7

Allegro

No. 8

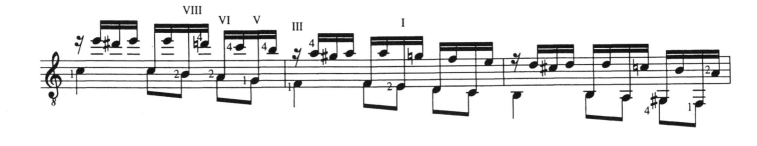

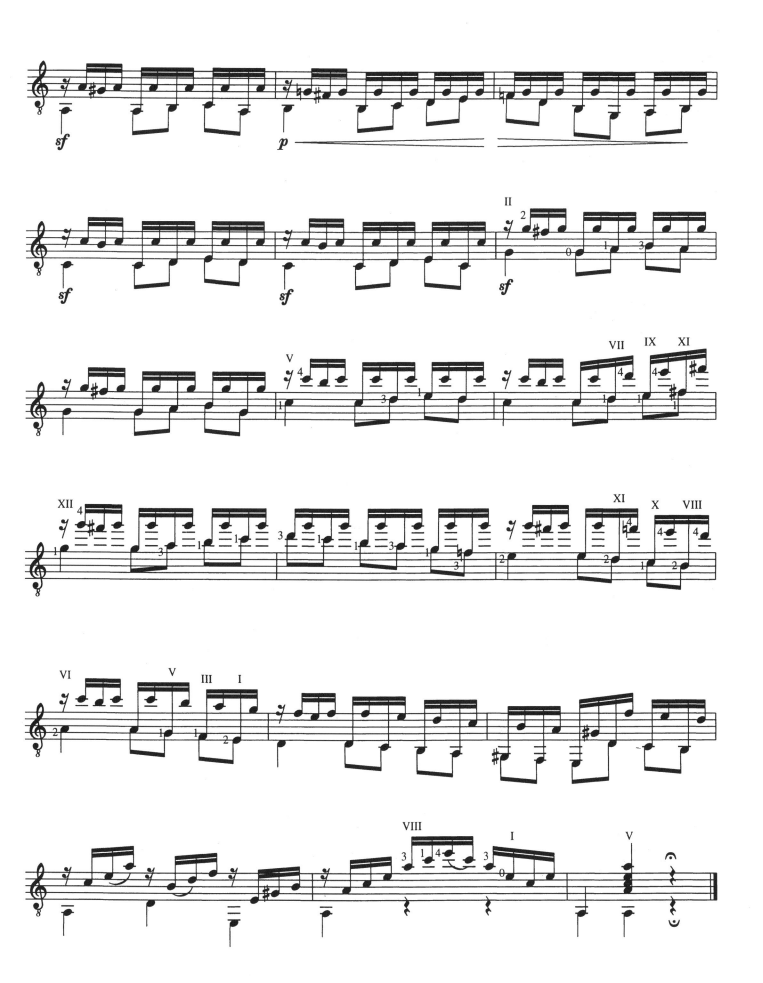

67

No. 9

68

No. 14

75

No. 16

Allegro maestoso

77

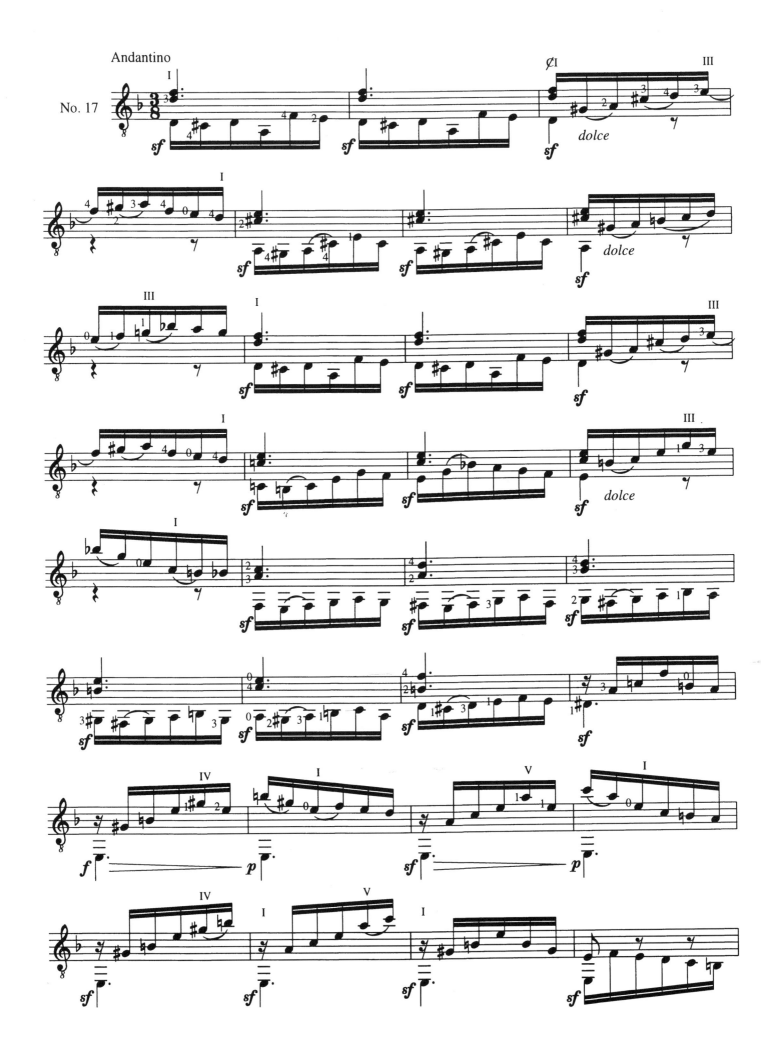

No. 17

78

No. 18

Con brio

Grazioso

No. 20

83

Allegro maestoso

No. 22

84

85

Allegro con moto

No. 23

86

XVIII Leçons Progressives
(18 Progressive Lessons)
for the Guitar

Opus 51

This page has been left blank to avoid page turns within pieces.

No. 3

Agitato

94

No. 4 Maestoso

No. 5 Andantino

95

No. 6

Grazioso

No. 8

98

Allegretto

No. 9

No. 10

Allegretto

No. 11

No. 13

Allegretto

No. 16

Presto

Grazioso

No. 18

108

Studii Dilettevoli
(Entertaining Studies)

or Collection of Various Original Pieces
for the Guitar

Opus 98

This page has been left blank to avoid page turns within pieces.

Andantino

No. 1

Allegro

No. 2

115

This page has been left blank to avoid page turns within pieces.

Larghetto

No. 3

No. 4

118

This page has been left blank to avoid page turns within pieces.

Andantino

No. 5

Allegro

No. 6

Andantino

No. 7

Etudes Instructives Faciles et Agreables
(Easy and Agreeable Instructive Etudes)
for the Guitar

Comprising an Album of
Cadences, Caprices, Rondos and Preludes

Opus 100

Cadences

131

No. 5

Andantino

134

Caprices and Rondos

Allegro

No. 11
Caprice

140

142

No. 13
Caprice

Affettuoso

144

No. 14
Caprice

146

No. 15
Rondo

Allegro

148

149

No. 16
Rondo

Allegretto

Preludes
to use as cadenzas before beginning a piece of music

No. 23

(Allegro)

157

Prime Lezioni Progressive
First Progressive Lessons
for the Guitar
(Part One)

Opus 139

Andantino

No. 1

Grazioso

No. 2

No. 3

(Allegretto)

Maestoso

No. 4

Andantino

No. 5

Allegretto

No. 6

Other Mel Bay Guitar Solo Books

The Baroque Guitar in Spain and the New World (Koonce)
65 Gradually Progressive Pieces and 6 Studies from Opus 241 by Carulli (Roberts)
Anthology of 19th Century Studies (Beck/Postlewate)
Chopin for Acoustic Guitar (R. Yates)
The Complete Chopin Mazurkas (Aron)
Edvard Grieg: 16 Lyric Pieces (R. Yates)
Franz Schubert Arranged for Guitar (Calderon)
The Guitar Transcriptions of Francisco Tárrega (Ballam-Cross)
J. K. Mertz: Original Compositions for Classic Guitar (Reuther)
Johannes Brahms: Hungarian Dances for Solo Guitar (Eötvös)
La Melanconia by Mauro Giuliani (arr. by P. Romero)
Masters of Russian Composition: Alexander Borodin and Anatoly Lyadov (arr. by R. Mamedkuliev)
Padovec Collection (Dojcinovic)
Parlor Gems (Mayes)
Peer Gynt Suite: Op. 46 (Plus Solveig's Song) (R. Yates)
Selected Operatic Fantasies of Mertz (Torosian)
Woodland Sketches: The Music of Edward MacDowell (R. Yates)
Best of Bach (Castle)
Easy Classic Guitar Solos (Castle)
Treasures of the Baroque Volume 1 (Grimes)
Treasures of the Baroque Volume 2 (Grimes)
Treasures of the Baroque Volume 3 (Grimes)
Favorite Hymns for Classical Guitar (Castle)
Essential Bach: Arranged for the Guitar (Afshar)
Scarlatti and Weiss for Guitar (Afshar)
Spanish Composers for Classical Guitar (Afshar)
Valses Poeticos by Enrique Granados (Afshar)
25 Etudes Esquisses for Guitar (Garcia)
Andrew York: Three Dimensions for Solo Guitar
Anthology of Dimitri Fampas Music for Guitar (E. Fampas)
Classic Koshkin (Koshkin/Koonce)
Contemporary Anthology of Solo Guitar Music (Postlewate)
Contemporary Guitar Composers of the Americas (Multiple Authors)
Conversation Pieces (Long)
Diego Barber Compositions for Classical Guitar
Guitar Compositions by Carlos Dorado
Homage to Villa-Lobos and Other Compositions (Postlewate)
Introspect (Pellegrin)
Lyrical Solos (W. Bay)
Master Anthology of New Classic Guitar Solos (Multiple Authors)
Solos for Guitar (F. Hand)
The Contemporary Guitar: An Anthology of New Music (S. Yates)
The Jovicic Collection (Dojcinovic)
Well-Tempered Blues (Beauvais)

WWW.MELBAY.COM